THE DEATH

OF

CUPID

THE DEATH
— OF —
C U P I D

Reclaiming the wisdom of love,
dating, romance and marriage

Nachum Braverman & Shimon Apisdorf

LEVIATHAN PRESS
BOOKS THAT MAKE A DIFFERENCE

The Death of Cupid
Reclaiming the wisdom of love, dating,
romance and marriage
by Nachum Braverman & Shimon Apisdorf

Leviathan Press
2505 Summerson Road
Baltimore, MD 21209
(410) 653-0300
Fax (410) 653-1984

ISBN 1-881927-07-5

Printed in United States of America / First Edition
Cover Illustration by Julius Ciss (416) 784-1416
Cover and jacket design by Lightbourne Images © 1996
Page layout by Fisherman Sam
Author Photos: Nachum by Manny Saltiel / Shimon by
Miriam Apisdorf
Technical Consultants:E.R./D.L./Y.B.Z.

All Leviathan Press books are available at bulk order dis-
counts for educational,promotional and fundraising pur-
poses.

Acknowledgments

I have been blessed with wise and gifted teachers: Rabbi Noah Weinberg, Rabbi Yaacov Weinberg and Rabbi Yosef-Chaim Meyer. If the publication of this book served only to acknowledge my debt to them: *Dayenu*. This would have been enough.

Nancy Lee typed and retyped the original manuscript more times than I like to think. The Almighty should remember her for good and answer all her prayers.

Shimon Apisdorf, my co-author, is my paradigm of a righteous man. It has been a privilege to work with him on this book.

My students over the years taught me, I believe, far more than I taught them.

Thanking Emuna, my wife, is difficult. How do you thank your heart? I owe her more than I can say.

Nachum

For Emuna

Acknowledgments

The following people, each in their own way, made an invaluable contribution to this book. Ann Sinclair, Sharon Goldinger, Robyn Holliday, Shlomo Horowitz, Julie Mednick, Russell Simmons, Rabbi Asher Resnick, Amy Greenberg, Malka Levine, Rebbetzin Twerski, Ann Apisdorf, Auntie and Arthur.

As always, my loving family.

My incredible children. Esther Rivka, Ditzah Leah and Yitzchak Ben Tzion.

My wife Miriam. Still the best editor I know and truly the woman of my dreams.

The Almighty. Source of all blessing.

Shimon

*T*he truth is that Cupid should be seen as Public Enemy Number One.

CONTENTS

INTRODUCTION

−1−

THE WISDOM OF ᴍARRIAGE

−2−

THE WISDOM OF *D*ATING

−3−

THE WISDOM OF *S*EX

—4—

THE WISDOM OF ROMANCE

INTRODUCTION

The Death of Cupid: Long Live Love

If ever there were a symbol for true love, the symbol would be Cupid. And just who is this Cupid? Is he an angel? A devil in disguise? Certainly he is adorable as only a baby can be. Plump, squeezable, charming and wonderfully innocent—except for that bow and arrow in his hands.

But don't let that baby face fool you. Behind Cupid's comely eyes lies all the formidable power one would expect from a veritable god, which is exactly what Cupid is. Cupid is none other than the son of Mercury, god of commerce, and Venus, goddess of love. Cupid himself is the god of love.

Cupid is a playful god who likes to scamper about shooting tender golden-tipped arrows. His arrows gracefully fly through the air carrying with them the promise of eternal happiness. Once struck, the objects of Cupid's aim are overcome by a desire so passionate, and a love so fiery, that they can never be extinguished. No one in the world could be more fortunate than two people shot through the heart with Cupid's arrow. The bliss that awaits those who have been so blessed by the god of love is beyond what anyone could ever dream of.

And what does the future hold for this love-struck couple? Certainly there will be long periods of staring dreamily into one another's eyes. They will be surrounded by an almost mystical aura—a glow—whenever they are together. They will be the best of friends and the best of lovers. They will always be supportive and draw hope, courage and inspiration from one another. Their shared existence will be, in a word, perfect: endlessly fulfilling, impassioned and happy beyond belief.

Alas, perfection is an illusion, and Cupid is a myth (and a very stubborn myth at that). The ancient gods have long been relegated to the dustbins of history, yet this vision of idyllic love is something that many secretly—and not so secretly—still search for. There is a part of our culture's psyche that refuses to let go of the mythical vision of love that Cupid symbolizes. So we continue to honor it—in film, art and music; on greeting cards; and in hundreds of romance novels that sell millions of copies every year. So the myth goes on. At one time or another we have all dreamt of being a victim of Cupid's arrow, but that's a problem—because as we know, there is no Cupid and there are no potion-tipped enchanted arrows.

But if there is no Cupid, what is there? There is still the very real power of love, even without Cupid; there is the possibility for a deeply fulfilling married life; for a life filled with passion and intimacy. And in real life, these can be achieved— if only we would finally put Cupid to rest.

The truth is that Cupid should be seen as Public Enemy Number One. Rather than embracing him, it's time we turned on him. Love, dating, marriage, romance and intimacy are vital parts of real people's lives in the real world. To stand a chance of experiencing all we want in life, we need to exorcise our myths and fantasies and replace them with real-world wisdom—wisdom that refuses to deny the heart its dreams and brings the real and the ideal together—which is what this book is all about.

The Death of Cupid is about reclaiming some of life's most essential wisdom. It's about how a light from the past can illuminate our present and our future.

The wisdom this book seeks to reclaim and share flows from ancient Jewish texts and perspectives on many of life's core issues—and these are timeless. The issues we will discuss include pain and pleasure, fulfillment and emptiness, the need for introspection, life goals and the forging of character. Of course they also include love, dating, physical intimacy, romance and marriage.

The Power of Definitions

The beginning of wisdom is the definition of terms.

Socrates

Each of the four sections in *The Death of Cupid* begins with a definition, because sound, workable definitions are essential to grasping and applying wisdom to our daily lives. Let's look at friendship as an example. If two people have different definitions of friendship and both consider the other to be a friend, then what will likely transpire is a confusing and frustrating experience. Each will bring a different set of expectations and assumptions to the relationship, each will invest different amounts of emotional energy into the relationship and each will be caught off guard when reciprocity seems to be out of kilter. The result will be a friendship gone bitter, and the cause will have been different views of what a friendship was supposed to be all about in the first place.

As you travel through the pages of *Cupid*, you will encounter radical definitions of love, dating, marriage, romance and even sex. These definitions will challenge you to rethink some of your most basic assumptions and will reveal new paths for achieving dimensions of love, commitment, closeness, passion and intimacy that you thought might only be the stuff of dreams.

Wisdom: The Eye of the Storm

We are keenly aware that life today is vastly different from what it was just forty years ago. The decades and eras of history are like successive seasons of hurricanes: each brings unpredictable winds that thrash violently about. Each has its own identity, and each leaves its own legacy. Yet to each storm there is a calm and tranquil eye. Even amidst the unceasing winds of change, there is an ageless core. This core is wisdom, a constant and calming presence.

We live in the midst of an unusually violent storm. Marriage and much that goes with it— love, dating, parenting, sexuality, romance and commitment—are no longer what they once were. We are often bewildered. We feel disoriented and stagger about like survivors searching for familiar shards to link us to a more familiar time.

The storm in America looks like this. Half of all marriages today end in divorce.[1] Of those that do endure, how many are truly happy?

The storm continues. Most people who get divorced look to marry again.[2] And of those who remarry, most end up divorced again. Every year a million kids experience divorce.[3] Yet, despite the trends, people try to remain hopeful. They still date and seek out love and romance, marriage, family, stability and happiness. They hope that somehow they will be different.

This then is the place for wisdom—here, amidst a raging storm born of heartless statistics. Wisdom is hopeful because it has weathered many a storm, optimistic because it has seen great joy and even buoyant because it knows that there is life beyond endurance and that there can even be happiness. In *The Death of Cupid* we will be sharing insights that will bolster your hopes for love and help you build a reality out of your dreams.

This book comes with no promises or guarantees (unlike Cupid's arrow) because in life, as we know, there are no guarantees. In life there are three ingredients for success: wisdom, effort and prayer. In *The Death of Cupid* we will share some of the essential wisdom necessary to understand, find and achieve a loving, happy, passionate and fulfilling marriage. It's up to you to provide the effort, which will need to be considerable. As for the prayer, you may as well begin now, and hopefully your prayers will soon be answered.

The
Wisdom
of
Marriage

– 1 –

The Wisdom of Marriage

The Means and the Ends of Marriage

*T*he goal of marriage is life. Let's take a look.

> *Not too long ago a couple came to Nachum for counseling. "These were two intelligent, very together people teetering on the edge of divorce. Jenny wanted a few more years to achieve what her education had prepared her to achieve, and Stuart wanted to start building a family. I still remember Jenny's words—'Why in the world would you think I'd suddenly jeopardize what I've accomplished by*

> *having a baby now? Does it really mat-*
> *ter if we're only able to have one kid and*
> *not two?' If ever there was an instance of*
> *two opposing sets of values running*
> *headlong into one another, this was it. I*
> *asked them, 'Didn't you discuss this*
> *before you got married?' Their response*
> *came in the form of a blank stare, so I*
> *thought we needed to go back to square*
> *one."*

To life. To an understanding of marriage as a means and not an end. As something deep, rich, intimate, transcendent and beautiful, but a means nonetheless. Many people look forward to marriage as a time when their inner-life will be filled with a sense of calm and tranquillity, when the love that fills their hearts will make all of life's difficulties bearable and bring ultimate meaning to their existence. Marriage, they imagine, is bliss. They see marriage as a goal that brings with it happiness, contentment and most everything that life in the single's lane is lacking. This just isn't the case. No realization is more critical than the awareness that marriage in and of itself is not a life goal but rather a supremely potent vehicle for achieving life goals.

Marriage enables us to pursue the goals that give meaning to our lives with a drive, energy and effectiveness not available from any other source. Marriage is a unique resource that creates an expanded sense of being and potential while providing a wellspring of insight into self, others and life.

A person who is depressed, aimless and single and who then marries will be depressed, aimless and married. Only on the big screen do two lovers find that the passion of their love is enough to provide meaning, fulfillment and blissful contentment. Only in a fantasy does marriage have the ability to become a pulsating relationship that provides all of life's emotional sustenance and satisfies every existential need.

In real life an unbearable strain is placed on a relationship when it is expected to fulfill all of life's loftiest aspirations, lay to rest the disquieting questions that tug at every human soul and provide an ultimate sense of fulfillment and happiness.

Real people in the real world need life goals. They need to be devoted to something beyond themselves and one another; they need ideals to pursue and they need dreams. To be married without having life goals is like being all dressed up with no place to go. To be married and to share a vision shaped by common ideals and dreams is to embrace a path of boundless potential.

The Definition of Marriage

Many of the obstacles that wound and even cripple a marriage are a direct result of a faulty definition of marriage. Today, marriage seems to be a kind of evolutionary accident. After a period of getting acquainted, dating and becoming romantically involved comes the stage of restlessness. This is where a couple confronts one of life's most terrifying questions: Now what? With the only answer to "Where do we go from here?" being marriage, this innocent couple ends up wedged between the panic, split and run ("a part of me will always love you" routine) and deciding to take the only available next step. This next step lands them on the altar of marriage vowing to share their lives—their joys and sorrows—"till death do us part." The only thing missing is "and they all lived happily ever after." Because these days, most of them don't.

For many couples the problem begins with a mistaken notion of what marriage is exactly. Jewish wisdom defines marriage as the commitment a man and a woman make to become one and to pursue together common life goals.

Jewish wisdom assesses the highest priority to clarifying life goals. A clear idea of one's life goals is the surest foundation for meaningful, productive, spiritual living and forms the bedrock for a fulfilling marriage as well. Life goals also create a context for living that enables couples to put other matters into perspective. Couples may argue over a stray toothpaste cap, the style of a new couch or whose turn it is to get up with the baby, but no matter how heated these run-ins become, they should never destroy a marriage. Remember this rule of thumb: a marriage that is threatened by where to spend a vacation is a marriage that lacks the bond of common life goals.

Marriages dissolve when two lives are pointed in different directions. Conflicts over the color of a new kitchen can generally be resolved, but conflicts in direction often cannot. Couples rarely break up over clashes in taste, but they do break up over whose career comes first when the two conflict. Couples will break up over whether to give priority to career or family, over whether or not to have children, over the education of their children and over which religion or how much of it to have in the home. These, and other issues like them, are anything but trivial. These are life goal issues. They are issues every individual needs to carefully consider before inviting someone else to share his or her life. Two people who don't know where they are going should never commit to getting there together.

There is another reason why life goals need to be carefully considered in the context of marriage: marriage is primarily a shared life experience. In this sense the relationship that marriage creates needs to be understood as an entity whose sum is greater than the two individuals involved. Two people can't successfully create a life together unless they share a clear and mature sense of the kind of life they want to build. This goes far beyond what type of house they hope to live in, where they would like to eat and what type of music they want to listen to. Both partners need to know what values they want their shared life to represent because this is what marriage is—a shared life. They need to have a vision of the ideals they want to express in the way they spend their money and their discretionary time. And they need to know what type of character (in addition to career) they want their children to possess.

If you want to go to the beach, you can't share a car with someone who wants to go skiing. If you want stability in life, you've got to have goals. In marriage, shared goals bring stability, structure and harmony. They are also the basis for fulfillment and a catalyst for the deepest of loves.

If You Died Tomorrow

Life goals are those things you'd regret not having done if you died tomorrow. When it comes to life goals, the problem is that most of us have never been encouraged to consider them—at least not in a deliberate, thoughtful and ongoing manner.

There is no course on life goals offered in high school or college. You won't find a life goals channel on cable television, your boss won't encourage you to think about them on the job and there is no apparent connection between clear life goals and your capacity to earn an ever heftier salary.

Nonetheless, the issue of life goals is one we simply cannot afford to overlook. Establishing goals is a necessity, not a luxury.

Everyone has moments when life goal questions flash in and out of one's mind, though these questions rarely receive their due attention. We're too busy living and trying to get ahead to think about where we really want to go. On occasion, usually in the setting of a late night conversation, issues of life goals do make their way into our discussions. As enlightening and inspiring as these after-hour talks may be, by the next morning they have often fallen victim to the relentless pursuit of whatever it was we were pursuing before we stopped to consider the broader context of our lives.

And it's no wonder. After all, we spend years learning how to make a living but rarely consider how much money we actually need to live. We assume we can never have too much, and thus we are constantly in pursuit of more. Why we need all that buying power, in what way those possessions actually enhance our lives and whether priorities exist that supersede our financial goals are questions we are rarely challenged to confront.

In some vague sense, everyone knows what he or she wants in life. Everyone wants to be happy, to be good, to have friends, to raise a family and to see a better world. These are lovely sentiments, but they certainly aren't what paves the path to success today. In the words of Gloria Steinem, *"We best know our values when we look at our check stubs."* The truest indication of our values and goals isn't in what we say—it's in how we spend our time and money that speaks loudest about who we are. The most accurate picture of what we truly care about is painted by the way we live.

To Choose or Not to Choose: The Choice Is Yours

It is very important to have conviction behind your decisions. If you do not, someone else will fill the gap.

Rowland Perkins—Founding partner, Creative Artists Agency, Inc.[4]

In truth it is very rare to find a person who has no goals. But who has determined what our goals ought to be? If we fail to grapple with values and define goals, then by default the prevailing cultural currents in society will define our goals for us. And society's standard, the great and elusive goal toward which we are all propelled, can be summed up in one word: Success. *People* magazine is filled with the lives of the rich and the famous, not the fulfilled and the happy. One advertisement for a sleek import car showed a desert sun setting behind the automobile. The caption read: "You are looking at 3,500 pounds of life goal fulfillment."

While we may react to this assertion as being absurd, someone on Madison Avenue knew better. And some corporation wagered a lot of money that this ad would strike a responsive chord in many Americans.

A corollary to success is career. Success is spelled m-o-n-e-y, and money is the objective of most career paths. Think about it. If someone says to you, "See that woman? She is a very successful attorney," what do you think "successful" implies? Does it mean that she is a particularly skilled interlocutor or that she donates a great deal of her services to needy individuals and institutions? Of course not! Though all of these things may be true, what is implied in the word "successful" is *rich.* By and large our culture has come to define success in monetary terms.   As the philosopher George Santayana observed, *"The American talks about money because that is the symbol and measure he has at hand for success, intelligence and power."* *Successful* is a euphemism for wealthy. And since our careers (and the paychecks and perks that come with them) are the way to realize our goal of being successful, we inevitably come to see what we do for a living as opposed to *what we do while we're living* as the defining element of our existence.

In the Jewish view of life, careers are seen as a necessary evil, not the defining element of personal identity. Way back in the Garden of Eden when Adam and Eve ate from the Tree of Knowledge, they were told, *"Now you will eat bread by the sweat of your brow."* Until that moment, no one had to earn a living. The long hard path to achieving professional and financial success is a curse, not a source of meaning and fulfillment that deserves so much of our life's energy. There is far more to life than making a living and much more to personal identity than can be squeezed onto a business card.

Forever remember that the business of life is not merely about business, but about life.

B.C.Forbes—Founded*Forbes* magazine in 1917, "to promulgate humanness in business, then woefully lacking."

The western world has been had. We have allowed ourselves to be convinced that the curse of a career is to be the ambition of our lives. It's as though we are working for a final epitaph that would read, "Author of a thousand briefs, filler of a thousand teeth." True, every job involves some sort of service to individuals and society, but there has got to be more to life than a career. Only the very fortunate do work that is stimulating and challenging, promotes personal growth, leaves them with their dignity intact and affords a sufficient livelihood to pursue deeper life goals. Only the tiniest fraction of people find true fulfillment through their professions. The rest of us are left to trudge through the years looking forward to weekends and vacations that are but brief bridges of respite to more of the same drudgery.

In addition to their trivialization of life, career and success as life goals pose another problem: they make for lousy marriages. While striving to be a millionaire by forty doesn't inevitably lead to a watered-down family life, it certainly doesn't help. Success at anything takes time, work, energy and concentration. The massive investment of all these resources into a career leaves people with little capital to invest at home.

Nachum meets regularly with business people in their offices to study Jewish wisdom.

"Once, during one of our weekly study sessions, I told Herb and Bob that they were so preoccupied with their work that they could barely pay attention to our discussion. Well, that just opened up the floodgate, and our whole conversation turned to their irreconcilable tensions of work versus relaxation, work versus family and work versus life. 'It's not like you guys are just starting out,' I said. 'You're both very successful already. Why don't you spend more time studying and with your families?'

'We plan to,' they assured me. 'We just need to reach a certain plateau, and that's exactly what we'll do."

People don't set out to make their job the center of their lives or tell themselves, "I'm going to work compulsively until the day I die." It just ends up that way. After reaching one plateau, they realize that for a little more investment of effort they will be able to reach another plateau, and then another and another and another.

No one dies with half their desires satisfied.

Elijah of Vilna

People rationalize that they need to make a lot of money so that later in life they'll have the time and ability to do the things they really want to do. They defer living until retirement while years are spent preparing for some sort of grand finale to life. Sadly, when the time comes, they don't know what they want to do, and like so many millionaire lottery winners, they end up back where they started—at work.

Life comes with certain facts. One of the facts of life is that many of the most important aspects of living just can't be deferred. The frenzied race for career advancement, success and the acquisition of a solid portfolio comes at a price—a price few of us can afford to pay. You can't reraise your children or grow close to your spouse after spending the time needed for those things in your office. The notion that life starts only after retirement is total capitulation to a set of goals that robs our life of many of its most precious moments. One woman lamented to Nachum that her husband was retiring and had promised they would now have plenty of time to spend together. *"When the children were growing up and I needed him, he wasn't around. Now I'm no longer interested in spending time with him."*

Despite everything we just said about career and wealth and priorities, we need to add that there is nothing wrong with success per se; it's the way we have come to relate to success that often proves to be problematic. Success needs to be understood for what it is: a means and not an end. Success, wealth, status and all sorts of eyebrow-raising acquisitions are wonderful, but they are not what life is all about. What's more, not only is success not a meaningful life goal, it's also not a goal that lends itself to the deepening of a couple's relationship. Can the joint pursuit of money draw a man and woman together in a deep and lasting way? Can we say that what unites us is the mutual desire to be well dressed, wealthy and tan? These things are nice, but they are only the spice of life, not the main course. And no one is satisfied for long with a plate garnished only with spices.

After finishing his degree in accounting, Todd did two years of graduate work in international politics before leaving school to open a pretzel franchise that catered to the particular tastes of undergrads. Two franchises and one very successful business later, Todd is now a mid-size venture capitalist with a good eye for what sells and a voracious appetite for late night TV sports. Julie, his wife, is not. Julie is an elementary school music teacher with a love for antique shops and has no idea that a football isn't round.

"Don't ask us what we have in common," Todd said, "you're liable to make us realize something that's better we didn't realize." Then after reflecting for a moment, "You know what it is?" Todd asks rhetorically, "it's all those nights we volunteer at the soup kitchen—especially on Thanksgiving—that's why our

> marriage is so solid. It really doesn't matter to us if our kids go into business, academics or whatever. We just hope they know where to spend their Thanksgiving nights. Isn't that what it's all about anyway?"

Goals That Bind

We defined life goals as those things you would regret having not done if you died tomorrow. We would now like to offer two brief examples of life goals (this whole topic is dealt with in greater depth on pages 73-79) and explore how they work to foster togetherness, intimacy and mutual fulfillment.

Goal #1

I don't want to be the same person at the end of my life that I was when I was twenty. I want to use my strengths in a productive manner. I'd like to make progress in dealing with my shortcomings and weaknesses. I'd like to be as concerned about others as I am about myself, and I'd like to broaden my understanding of myself, human nature and life. In short, I want my life to be an ongoing process of growth and development.

This is an admirable goal indeed. In fact the legendary eighteenth-century sage, Rabbi Elijah of Vilna, summed up the Jewish view of this goal when he said, *"If life isn't a process of personal development, then what could be the purpose of living?"*

When two people relate to marriage as a partnership in personal growth, they will build a life that draws upon all their creativity and drives them to pursue new insights wherever possible. When each spouse is devoted not only to his or her own growth but also to tenderly encouraging his or her partner's growth, then their shared life becomes an adventure at least as exciting as one invested in building a new business. When two people have one another's best interests in mind, when they encourage one another out of love and not for the sake of any hidden agenda, then a symbiosis emerges that fuses two souls in the deepest way imaginable.

Goal #2

I would like to get married, have children, raise a nice family and be a productive member of my community.

This goal is simple, straightforward and, from the perspective of Jewish wisdom, quite profound.

If you conceive of, design and then develop a new product that finds a successful niche in the market, will you not have a feeling of great satisfaction? If this product enabled doctors to treat certain diseases more successfully, would you not experience a great sense of fulfillment? What if you had a partner in that achievement? Would the two of you not have a unique bond that would always tie you to one another?

This model provides us with an appreciation of one way that Judaism views the family. Jewish wisdom understands having children and raising a family as part of our responsibility to humanity. The opportunity to raise children is the privilege of having the chance to develop a product that can walk out into the marketplace of civilization and make a meaningful contribution—whether that contribution is to the life of "just" one other person, to a community or to all of mankind.*

Be fruitful and multiply.

Genesis 1:27

After creating the first human beings, God made a point of telling them to reproduce and populate the world. Knowing human appetites and drives as we do, isn't it obvious that human beings would have done a good job at being fruitful and multiplying without God encouraging them to do so? Nobody had to tell the animals to procreate, and there are plenty of them around. This distinction is the very point of there being a specific Divine command to have children. Human procreation is meant to go far beyond the mere propagation of another one of the many species that inhabit the earth. Human reproduction is not a biological numbers game.

---

* The Talmud teaches, "He who saves a life is as if he saved an entire world." In a certain sense, the positive impact we may have on an individual is no less significant than an impact that touches masses of people. And that individual can even be ourselves.

There is a qualitative element in human child-bearing and family building that is meant to include a relationship with God. The spiritual and moral dimensions of every aspect of family life are what elevate human procreation and the human family to a unique plateau.

When it comes to the venture we call marriage, parenthood and the business of building a family become endeavors that bond a couple as little else can. As the partners in this venture strive to create a marriage and a home life that will in turn mold children who care about themselves and the world around them, they discover the deepest resources and potentials in both themselves and one another. This entrepreneurial process of family building takes reproduction out of the realm of the animal and transports it to the domain of the civilized, the spiritual and the human.

I have three pictures on my desk. One is of me with my parents. The other two are with my wife and sons on family vacations. I don't have any pictures of me at the office, working late, making the "deal," or going to black-tie dinners. I don't have a picture of me making a deposit at a bank-teller window, flying first-class to Tokyo, or returning a twenty-eight percent margin to my company. Just the family.

Richard Edler—Former president or managing director of three Los Angeles advertising agencies and author of *If I Knew Then What I Know Now.*[5]

A life directed by goals that we don't want to regret if they are left undone is a life that will likely produce riches beyond our wildest dreams. A marriage centered around such goals will be a marriage adorned with peerless beauty.

The Commitment Factor

"Mr. Brown," the doctor began, "your situation is worse than we anticipated. The best chance we have of saving your leg is by pursuing a series of operations. This will involve breaking and resetting a bone, removing all the infected tissue and performing a number of skin grafts. There will be intermittent periods of physical therapy, and you will have to radically alter your diet and lose at least fifty pounds. This is going to be a long process but with aggressive action, I believe there is a reasonable chance we can save your leg. And Mr. Brown, you need to make a decision soon, very soon. Otherwise there is a strong likelihood you will lose your leg."

Does anyone doubt what Mr. Brown will do? Is there much of a chance that he might respond by saying, "Listen, Doctor, the procedure you are describing is more than I can bear. Please amputate my leg; I just can't go through all that."

*The relationship of a husband and a
wife is like the relationship of the right
hand to the left hand.*

Chazon Ish—twentieth-century
talmudic sage.

We defined marriage as the commitment a
man and a woman make to become one and to
pursue together common life goals. We have also
discussed the invaluable dynamic that shared life
goals bring to marriage. The next question is,
what is the perspective regarding the nature of the
underlying commitment that constitutes a marriage? Commitments in life come in many shapes
and sizes. There is commitment to community or
country, and there is commitment to a favorite
team. There is commitment to a pet, to a business
partner and to a friend. What is it that two people
mean when they are committing to marriage?

The first thing the Bible teaches about marriage is that, through it, a man and a woman
"become one flesh."[6] To understand the meaning of

commitment in marriage is to understand Mr. Brown's commitment to his leg.

His commitment to his leg is vital and holistic in nature. He's not just committed to his leg; he is his leg. It would never occur to him to reconsider his commitment to his leg—not if it were scarred, ugly, broken, required painful surgery or even if he met someone who had much nicer legs. He would only seriously reconsider his commitment to his leg if gangrene had set in. This is the meaning of *"one flesh."* The commitment of marriage is until its killing you.

Most people have a sense that this is what commitment is all about. Perhaps that is why the contemplation of marriage has a way of striking terror in the hearts of the mightiest of men. Regardless of who utters them, the words "Will you marry me?" are capable of turning the most confident, self-esteem-filled person into a stammering, jello-kneed wad of confusion, because everyone knows that there are only two possible answers to that question. It's either yes or no. And yes means forever. Did anyone ever suppose that the one who "popped the question" meant "Will you marry me for a while?" Of course not. Everyone knows that "Will you marry me?"

means forever. And forever means commitment—real commitment.

To further understand the meaning of commitment in marriage, we must realize that commitment means complete acceptance. In marriage we drop our resistance and allow another person into our lives. This type of mutual acceptance implies far more than just spending the rest of our years together. Marriage enables us to achieve a state of inclusion where our very being becomes one shared experience.

What marriage creates is not unlike what happened when the United States purchased the Louisiana Territory from France. The United States was the United States both before and after the purchase of this vast area that stretched from the Mississippi to the Rocky Mountains. At the same time, a permanent and profound change had taken place. The contour and borders of the country were dramatically altered, and contained within these boundaries was a whole new world of resources and potentialities. One could still clearly identify the pre-purchase United States (its government, states and people). Nothing had changed and everything had changed.

Marriage also creates a new reality while simultaneously preserving that which preceded the union. It is by way of this newfound oneness that we experience another human being as essential to our very sense of self. This in turn expands the horizons of our self-awareness and self-interest to include the person we love and are married to. Thus marriage is something all together different from the socially sanctioned living together of a man and a woman.

The commitment to marriage is the commitment to a reality that says "our" needs and "my" needs are interchangeable. That which is essential to "my" sense of well-being is that which is essential to "our" sense of well-being. Though we are two human beings, there is a dimension of *ourness* that makes us inseparable and indistinguishable. Even if one of us is thousands of miles away on a business trip, the awareness that the sense of personal well-being has been enhanced or diminished in a spouse necessarily alters our own feelings of well-being. A threat to my spouse is a threat to myself no less than is a threat to my own leg, my own heart or my own peace of mind. My "I" in essence has become "we." Not that I have in any way lost or compromised myself. Rather, my "self" has become wonderfully—almost miraculously—expanded and profoundly enhanced.

All of this is alluded to when the Bible speaks of the creation of the first human beings.

> *And God created Man in His image, in the image of God <u>He created him</u>, male and female <u>He created them</u>.*

Genesis 1:27

When one reads this verse, it is difficult to discern whether it is addressing the creation of an individual male human being (*"And God created man...He created him"*) or whether it is talking about the creation of both a man and a woman (*"...male and female He created them."*). This difficulty is compounded when in the very next chapter we read:

And then God fashioned the rib that He had taken from the man into a woman, and He brought her to the man.

Genesis 2:22

Clearly, this verse is talking about the creation of the first woman. If this is the case, then who was the earlier verse referring to when it said, *"...male and female He created them"*?

It is from these verses that Jewish wisdom discovers the ultimate meaning of the oneness created through marriage. The early sages taught that the first human being was a single entity comprised of every element—physical, emotional and spiritual—that is found in the male and every element that is found in the female. Only after creating this unified human being did God then separate this original "man" into an individual male and female, and finally God reunited them, as it says *"...and He brought her to the man."*[7]

This then is the paradigm for marriage. Human identity in its truest and most complete form is that which includes a man and a woman as one being. A marriage is the reunion of two disparate elements—a man and a woman—that rightly belong together if they are to achieve a complete sense of self. Two people who commit to marry are committing to the fusion of their beings into a new and distinct entity.

The realization that this is what the commitment to marriage entails can be frightening. This is because marriage is fraught with all sorts of risks, particularly when it takes us to uncharted regions of emotional awareness and forces us to confront deep vulnerabilities. It doesn't take long for husbands and wives to discover one another's shortcomings and frailties. Though their bodies may be clothed, their hearts, minds and souls often stand fully exposed. At the same time, the commitment of marriage is also freeing because it creates ultimate security. The environment of two souls who have *become one flesh* is the safest place possible for personal and spiritual growth to take place. In marriage you don't have to pretend to be something you're not. Marriage is a nurturing emotional spa where a woman and man are lovingly devoted to one another's inner development. Ultimately it is where life goals become reality, dreams become the stuff of everyday living and love takes on a quality that defies articulation.

The Comfort of Divorce

From Woodstock and the Age of Aquarius until the takeover of the personal computer and the era of HIV, our culture has seen wave after wave of new attitudes toward relationships, lifestyles and marriage. There was a time when society's ideal marriage was a lifelong monogamous relationship. While this is still most people's ideal, and all new couples' dream, it is no longer the norm. We have reached a point where more marriages end in divorce than don't and where more divorcees remarry than don't. Lifelong monogamous relationships have become the exception to the rule. As a result we now live in a reality that says although romantics may dream of one type of life, the emergent norm has become not only short-lived marriages but repetitive short-lived marriages.

Jewish wisdom sees divorce as a valid option that takes the harsher side of life into full consideration. The understanding of marriage as a man and a woman being *one flesh* also recognizes that marriages can enter gangrenous cycles in which divorce becomes the best option. At the same time, it is not gangrene that ends many marriages today but rather an awfully big headache. Just like marriage seems to be a natural next step in an evolving relationship, divorce has become a common place of refuge when "the excitement just isn't there anymore." While some relationships fall completely apart, others just fizzle out when two people get tired of one another. When this occurs, one or both parties do what we are all inclined to do when we get bored—head for the exit. This is particularly true when no children are involved.

A marriage suffering from a lack of excitement, great sex, fun, romance, "good times just doin' nothing together" or all of the above certainly needs urgent attention, but it is far from terminal. If someone told you he had decided to amputate a leg because "there just isn't any fun left in it anymore," you would know he was crazy. The same thing is true of marriage. The fact that this "missing spark" leads to the dissolution of so many marriages reveals a great deal about our attitudes toward the inevitable vicissitudes of life.

The Pain-Pleasure-Comfort Principle

To understand this readiness to abandon dis-appointing marriages, we need to consider an important distinction: the distinction between pleasure and comfort. Jewish wisdom relates to this distinction as one of life's most important principles for successful living.

We all know what comfort is. Leaving work early at the beginning of a long weekend is com-fortable. Falling asleep with a soft breeze coming in through the window or easing into a hot bath is comfortable. Marriage is not comfortable. Marriage is deeply pleasurable. Unlike comfort, however, it requires the exertion of enormous effort and the acceptance of disquieting times.

All of our most meaningful accomplishments and deepest pleasures in life demand the invest-ment of great effort. It takes pain, frustration and heroic perseverance to master a musical instru-ment, excel in athletics or succeed in business. The same is true when it comes to raising children, and the same is true in marriage. It takes a lot of work.

Marriage doesn't allow much room for hid-ing. You have to repeatedly discuss, listen, rediscuss, work out and rework out all sorts of differences in opinion, personality conflicts and other sundry problems. You need to understand yourself, your spouse and the unique reactions that occur when your diverse chemistries are blended together. You need the courage of a mountain climber, the endurance of a triathlete and the grace, poise and timing of a ballerina. In short, marriage demands no less than what it takes for an Olympian to win a gold medal—and Judaism believes that we've all got it in us.

In our entertainment-centered culture, Hollywood carries Cupid's banner aloft and does its best to persuade us that "true love" is painless. Katherine Hepburn and Spencer Tracy never fought. And when they did, it was charming and witty and the inevitable outcome was that they fell more deeply in love. Love and marriage is one of those confounding places in life where we all want to believe something that we know isn't true. A part of us wants to believe that all we have to do is find "the right person," that "special someone," and then all the work is over—that blissful harmony is assured and peaceful rapture will become the background music for everyday living.

The reality is very different.

You can marry the "right" person and get divorced, and you can marry the "wrong" person and have a wonderful marriage. The best marriages belong to people willing to accept the most discomfort and invest the most effort to make the marriage work. In every marriage there comes a time when you think "this person is so difficult and unreasonable that I just can't take it any longer!" It's at such moments that the future is decided. If you can take a deep breath, turn around and work it out, then you'll have a good—no, a great—marriage. If you are unsure if you are capable of the commitment it takes to turn difficulties around, then you may not be ready for marriage yet.

Remember, the distinction between pleasure and comfort is critical. We all want our marriages to be pleasurable, but when we expect them to be comfortable, we find ourselves running away when things get difficult. "It's just not working out" often means "I'm just not willing to bear the discomfort." If we're married, the marriage begins to fall apart. If we're not married, our quest for comfort will force us to opt for trivial relationships that demand little effort and offer scant reward and shallow pleasures.

The pain-pleasure-comfort principle comes down to this: pleasure and comfort are two entirely different things. Comfort is merely the absence of pain, while pain and effort are prerequisites for genuine pleasure. When you walk out on pain, you also walk out on pleasure. And when you stick with things despite the pain and effort involved, you can achieve the profoundest pleasures—in marriage as well as in life.

"Hey, I'm not bragging, but there are two women who would marry me tomorrow if I would leave my wife; but I won't. And it's not because of the kids or anything like that because we don't have any kids. And it's not because Stacey is the most gorgeous women around or even the most exciting person to always be with. It's because she's my wife and I love her, which to me is all the reason in the world."

Stan is thirty-eight, works out regularly and travels a lot as a manufacturer's rep for an electronics company. His wife Stacey is thirty-seven, works part-time in a bank and has been struggling with bouts of depression for six years. She recently had a malignant tumor removed.

The
Wisdom
of
Dating

– 2 –

The Wisdom of Dating

The Definition of Dating

*D*ating is the process through which one explores the potential for a permanent marital relationship. The most obvious implication of this definition is that if you are not interested in or ready for a long-term relationship, then you shouldn't be dating. Likewise, don't call things that aren't dates—dates. Mislabeling various social experiences as dating can lead to a lot of confusion because dating is a loaded word that brings with it ambiguous connotations. If your interest is in spending a couple of hours in someone else's company, then say so. Going out for a cup of coffee is casual socializing, going to see a new film with someone is sharing a pleasant experience and skiing with someone else is usually a lot more fun than skiing alone—but these are not necessarily dates. They are camaraderie.

Now we can understand why a definition for marriage is a vital prerequisite to dating. Though dating must precede marriage, one first needs to understand what marriage is all about in order to create a framework for successful dating.

Having defined dating, let us now contrast this perspective with alternative definitions of dating. While rarely articulated, these definitions represent approaches to dating that work to undermine the meaningfulness of the experience.

1. **Dating is a sport**. By extension, dates are trophies. With this approach, each date is seen as a way to boost one's self-esteem or to enhance one's image in the eyes of other people. By ticking off a list of all the impressive people you have dated, you make a clear statement about your own enviable status.

2. **Dating is a way to alleviate loneliness.** In this guise, dating assumes a form where it takes advantage of other people and can also be dangerous. Though no malice is intended, it's not fair

to date someone as a distraction from boredom or loneliness, particularly if the other person may be entertaining thoughts of a more serious relationship. Also, if two lonely people enjoy their time together and end up getting romantically involved, they run the risk of getting tangled up in a relationship that is not suited for marriage on one hand and painfully difficult to exit on the other.

3. **Dating is a way of getting sex.** If you're not married or not planning to get married, dating is clearly the best and most socially acceptable way to find an outlet for one's natural urges. There is logic to this thinking, but when a primary aim of dating is the sexual encounter, this leads to a reductionist view of people that sees potential dates as unidimensional objects instead of multi-dimensional human beings.

4. **Dating is a way of taking revenge on people of the opposite sex for the unhappiness of your own life**. Today, many singles who would like to marry have become cynical. They are frustrated and unhappy and blame their woes on men who can't make a commitment, men who want to go to bed on the second date, women who won't look at them if they're not earning a six-figure salary and so forth. People have become soured

by the whole dating scene and look to subtly get even by not returning calls, giving a false impression or being nasty for no reason. Our response to this: it's just not worth it. We become diminished; nothing is achieved; and while revenge may be sweet, it's also a step backward.

5. **Dating is a way of getting your mother off your back**. True, but there is an alternative. Explain to her that you read this great book about marriage, that you are giving a lot of thought to the meaning of commitment, that you've decided to undertake a process of clarifying your life goals and that you need some time to think about these issues before getting involved in a relationship. If she looks a bit nervous, calmly reassure her that you are okay—this is not a premature mid-life crisis and that you really do want to get married.

Much of the mass frustration surrounding dating today is a direct result of the confusion about what dating is supposed to be all about. When two people approach dating as the process through which they are attempting to identify a suitable partner for life, then a common frame of reference is created. The existence of this common frame of reference promotes open and honest communication unclouded by any hidden agendas.

It encourages communication that is emotionally prepared to probe important personal issues and, most importantly, to communicate about those matters—goals, aspirations, beliefs, convictions and values—that will most significantly impact the direction of a couple's life together. When other activities and intentions masquerade as dating, the result is confusing and often painful. If you are lonely, in need of a boost to your ego or suffering from a nagging mother, then by all means do something about it. But don't date; it just isn't meant to be a band-aid for so much of what ails us.

A Rose By Any Other Name

The funny thing about dating is that, while it pretends to be so many things that it isn't, it does remain the only credible means of finding a mate. If we know that marriage is the commitment a man and a woman make to become one and to pursue together common life goals, and if we know that dating is the process through which two people explore the potential for that commitment, then the next thing we need to do is look closely at the ingredients needed to create a healthy and productive context for dating.

The Essence of Dating

The ability to make a commitment to everything that marriage consists of turns on three essential questions.

1. Do we have **life goals** that we can share?
2. Does the person I am dating have the necessary **character traits** for us to build a successful life together?
3. Is there the necessary **chemistry** between us?

Let's take a look at each one of these.

1. Shared life goals

As we discussed earlier, life goals are those things you'd regret not having done if you died tomorrow. When all is said and done and people are getting up to eulogize your life in this world, what is it you would want them to say? When you can answer this question, then you know what your life goals are.

Life Goals 101

If you don't know where you're going, you'll probably end up somewhere else.

Yogi Berra

The next seven pages contain a self-directed mini-workshop of exercises designed to clarify life goals. These exercises are not meant to be the final word on sorting out the very personal issue of life goals; rather, they are a suggested starting point. If some of these exercises work for you, that's great. If they don't, then perhaps they can serve as the raw material for constructing personalized exercises that are more appropriate for you. In any case, while goals are essential for life as well as for marriage, it is not essential that you complete this mini-workshop before proceeding with the rest of this book. If you choose to save this section for another day, then you will want to continue your reading on page 80.

EXERCISE #1   The Self-Interview

Ask yourself the following questions. (Be sure to ask these questions out loud: just make sure that no one is listening.)

1. If I could afford to take a year off and do whatever I wanted, what would I do with that year?

_____

_____

2. When it comes to (choose one or more of the following: business, marriage, my profession, being a parent, being a friend, being a human being, life), I always want to be thought of as someone who—

_____

_____

_____

2A.   What kind of person would make the
            above statements?
    1)Someone who cares a lot about _____

_____

    2)Someone who isn't very concerned with—

_____

_____

    3)Someone whose priorities are—

_____

4)Someone who values _____

_____

5)Someone who believes in _____

_____

3. If it were guaranteed that I would be suc-
    cessful, I would—

                    _____

_____

_____

3A.What does this tell me about myself
    and my goals?

                    _____

_____

_____

_____

EXERCISE #2   Someday ...

1. Someday I would like to _____

_____

_____

2.Someday I hope _____

_____

_____

3. Someday I'm going to _____

_____

_____

_____

EXERCISE #3   Write Your Own Epitaph

Your tombstone can only fit thirty words. The first five are the same for everyone; you fill in the rest.*

Here lies a person who _____

_____

_____

_____

_____

_____

* If you are one of those expressive people, go ahead and write more, but remember, big stones are quite expensive.

EXERCISE #4   Regrets

We all have memories of things we should have done but didn't, and it gets in your way the rest of your life.

Dr. Marion P. Pritchard— A Dutch psychoanalyst now living in Vermont. At great risk to her own life, she hid a Jewish family during World War II and killed a Nazi collaborator who suspected their presence.

1. Make a list of two or three things you regret most in your life—

   _____

   _____

2. Make a list of two or three things that, if never done, you will regret for the rest of your life.

   _____

   _____

2. Character Traits

Three of the most important traits to look for in a potential spouse are kindness, loyalty and honesty.

Let's begin with kindness and with a point of clarification. To be kind and to be nice are two very different things. Someone who is nice acts in a pleasant and socially agreeable manner. For example, a nice person says good morning and inquires about your well-being, holds the door, picks up the tab and would never spit on your tie—which is nice. Kindness, however, means to be unselfish and genuinely concerned with the needs of others. A kind act is an act that flows from this concern.

We often ask people who attend our classes and seminars what they are looking for in a spouse. Time and again the response is that they want to marry someone who is nice, which is meaningless. The fact that someone is nice doesn't really tell you much about a person other than that he or she is polite, courteous and never spits on other people's ties. When it comes to dating, you only want to date nice people. However, niceness is not necessarily an indicator of kindness.

Though you will only want to date people who are nice, an important part of the dating process is to try and discover if this very nice person is also a kind person. In marriage, it's not just nice to have a spouse who is kind—it's essential.

Kindness, Loyalty and Honesty

When a person takes two aspirin for a headache, he or she is performing an act of kindness. We don't think of it in this way because we expect people to be naturally concerned with and responsive to their own needs. How about with children? When a parent gives medicine to a child with the flu, is that an act of kindness? It certainly is, only we don't think of it as such because we expect parents to be attuned and sensitive to their children's needs.

For a healthy human being, kindness to oneself is natural; so is kindness to one's children. Once we move beyond ourselves and our children, it becomes an effort to expand the parameters of our lives to include others in the field of those we relate to with a substantial degree of care and concern.

Kindness is indispensable in a prospective marriage partner because, as we discussed earlier, the essence of marriage is the fusion of two human beings into a new unified being. The presence of the trait of kindness is an indicator that the person you are dating has the capacity for this expansion of self. It's just not possible to build a life with someone whose world view contains little more than him or herself.

Loyalty

When you are looking for someone who is loyal, it means you are looking for someone who understands that the commitment of marriage is forever. Loyalty means you can trust, rely and count on someone. When something good happens, you will always try to include the other person in that good; when things get difficult, you will do whatever you possibly can to support and assist the other person.

Murderers, drug dealers and felons all receive letters and visitors in prison—if from no one else, then from their parents. This doesn't mean that these parents condone their children's behavior—

it just means that they will always be there for them. While a child may sadden, enrage, hurt or scare a parent; parents rarely disown their kids. Parents are loyal. Without loyalty there is no parent-child relationship, no friendship and no meaningful form of partnership.

A marriage without loyalty just isn't a marriage. It's two lone travelers temporarily sharing the same quarters. And no matter how beautifully appointed those quarters may be, it's a disaster waiting to happen.

Honesty

Like many of their contemporaries in medical school, Bruce and Helena were recreational drug users. A little pot on the weekends to relax, coke here and there for special occasions but nothing out of the ordinary—at least that's what they both thought.

After they married and Helena became pregnant, they decided to put that stage of life behind them. Occasionally Bruce would still get high, which didn't thrill Helena, but she knew the pressures he labored under as a resident. After four years and two children , Helena discovered an empty bottle of prescription amphetamines in one of Bruce's dresser drawers. He had been writing prescriptions for himself. The next two years became a sorrowful game of cat and mouse as Helena uncovered one lie after another. In the end, Bruce and his habit had nowhere left to hide.

Three years later: *The only thing deeper than Helena's anguish was her commitment to her husband. Eventually Bruce sought help, and he still attends regular meetings. Together, Helena and Bruce have rebuilt a beautiful marriage.*

There is a legal standard known as "truth in advertising." In the financial world, it goes under the title "truth in lending." In these areas, truth means not to hide or misrepresent anything that might affect the decision of a potential client or buyer. To be honest in these circumstances means more than thou shalt not tell a lie; it means *thou shalt not be misleading.*

Lies create a distorted picture of reality. People lie to themselves in order to avoid dealing with reality. People also lie to others when they fear the consequences of confronting reality; their fear may be of embarrassment, punishment or rejection. Lying creates an illusory world where consequences can be avoided. In a relationship like marriage or in the arena of dating, which is an exploratory prelude to marriage, lying enables people to present a false image of themselves.

Dishonesty in marriage is devastating. It distorts the relationship, it's manipulative and it will almost always be discovered. Once uncovered, dishonesty creates an atmosphere of suspicion and doubt that drives away the possibility of intimacy. How can you be intimate if you're not even sure who you are being intimate with?

Does this mean that in dating and marriage you must give a day-by-day, blow-by-blow account of everything you ever did in your life? Must every detail of your life be laid bare for your spouse or potential spouse to examine as he or she sees fit? Certainly not. The truth-in-marriage rule means that you must honestly represent the kind of person you are, not every act you have ever done. If you are a responsible, disciplined, hard-working person who once lost a ridiculous amount of money on a trip to Las Vegas, you don't have to embarrass yourself by revealing your stupidity to your spouse or potential spouse. If, however, you regularly spend a significant amount of time and money gambling, that's another story. To hide that is to hide an important piece of information that could well influence whether or how someone relates to you.

The honesty we seek in marriage is based on self-awareness and the willingness to be self-revealing—honest disclosure. In other words, for people to be honest about who they are, they must possess a good degree of emotional self-awareness. In addition to being self-aware, they must have the integrity to show themselves for what they really are. You can't develop a relationship with someone who doesn't know him or herself or who won't be honest with you. Both trust and genuine communication depend on mutual honesty. Without it, life becomes a charade.

Honesty and Privacy: Openness and Boundaries

We all need privacy. Some aspects of our lives are appropriate for public view and some are not. Some things we are willing to share with our friends at work, while others are reserved only for our closest confidants. The same is true in marriage. There are some things we only want to share with our spouses and other matters that we want to keep in the privacy of our own hearts.

This setting of boundaries works to create healthy islands of privacy in our lives. A special friendship is special and nurturing precisely because there are boundaries that say "parts of my life are open only within the confines of this friendship." When our private space is violated, we feel that the very core of our being has been assaulted.

Marriage is private. The very privacy of the relationship is a key factor in fostering the intimacy and connectedness that nurtures our lives as nothing else can. The elements of privacy and exclusivity that exist between a man and a woman bring a unique energy and emotion to their relationship.

At the same time, even within the close and most intimate domain of marriage, people need to maintain their own personal space, their own private inner life. As a rule, what you don't want to reveal you should not be urged to reveal. Where you know your spouse would rather you didn't see—you should not look. While marriage is the merging of two people into a distinctive entity, this does not mean that marriage demands that we abdicate our private selves. Marriage *is* the creation of a shared essence, but it is not the liquidation of individuality or of either individual's need for inner privacy.

One's need to nurture a private sense of self in no way violates honesty or compromises the marital dimension of being *one flesh*. Just the opposite. The respect of privacy promotes trust and a feeling of security that in turn creates an environment conducive to honesty and openness.

3. Chemistry

The third question that needs to be addressed in dating is chemistry. This is often the most confusing part of dating.

The first reason why chemistry is so confusing is that we are unclear about the role it's supposed to play and how important it is or isn't. Clearly, if you're not attracted to someone, you will have a hard time building a marriage together. On the other hand, being attracted to someone is an inadequate basis for launching a marriage. This is similar to liking the paint job on your car—it's no fun driving a car that you can't stand looking at, but you don't buy a car based on the paint job either.

At the root of the confusion about chemistry lies another terribly perplexing issue: love. Here the critical distinction that needs to be made is between love on one side and infatuation and romance on the other.

Falling In and Out of Love

To best understand this confusion, try asking any single person the following question: "Do you want to be in love with the person you marry?" The answer will always be yes. No one wants to marry someone he or she is not in love with; after all, isn't it love that makes marriage so special? Fine. Now ask a second question: "Have you ever been in love?" This time only ninety-nine percent of the people you survey will answer yes. People fall in love. It seems to happen to just about everyone. The confusing and frightening part is this: people also fall out of love.

The phenomenon of falling in and out of love inevitably confounds singles and married people alike. If you're single, it works like this: "Of course I want to marry someone I'm in love with, but I know that people tend to fall out of love with the people they are in love with. This being the case, how can I know that the person I fall in love with and marry won't one day become the person I married and fell out of love with?" How can two people ever know if their love will last?

If you're married, it works like this: "I can't tell you exactly when it happened, but there is no denying that the magic spark isn't there any more. I just don't feel that we're in love the way we once were." And if you're not in love, where does that leave your marriage?

The problem here is that when people talk about falling in and out of love, what they are really talking about is romance and infatuation, not love. While romance has an important part to play in marriage, it isn't love.

The Definition of Love

Love is a deeply pleasurable emotion that grows out of identifying beauty, virtue and strength of character in another human being.

Don't believe a word that Cupid says: love is not blind. Beyond the instinctual parental bond, parents love their children because, more than anyone else, they see the beauty and goodness in the child. This is true whether the child is two, twenty or fifty years old. Likewise, that same parent who perceives every last vestige of quality in her child is also keenly aware of the child's less flattering qualities. Love is not blind; it's a microscope. Infatuation is blind.

Infatuation has a lot to do with desire and very little to do with a genuine recognition of who someone is. Love is a state in which senses of perception are finely tuned. Infatuation induces a dream-like state in which everything seems to be perfect and faults, if they exist at all, are "cute and adorable—somehow they are a part of what makes him or her so right."

The next time someone you're dating says, "I love you," look him right in the eyes and ask, "Why do you love me?" You can't love another person until you know that person. If you don't understand someone's character and aren't aware of his strengths and faults, you can't love him— but you can be very infatuated and easily become romantically involved.

Romance has its own ingredients, such as quaint French restaurants, flowery notes of adoration and endless moments staring longingly into one another's eyes. A lack of knowledge about who the other person is presents no barrier to involvement in the most romantically enchanting encounters.

Next time you find yourself falling in love, ask yourself what it is you are focusing on. And realize that saying "I'm in love" with someone you don't know is like saying you love a movie you've only seen the previews for.

Superficial Attraction

The second reason chemistry is so confusing is because there are a lot of things that attract us to someone—things that are appealing but that are not the person. Because we live in an age where so much of our identity is wrapped up in what we do for a living, it's no wonder that as we search for identity in others our eyes are naturally drawn to their resumes.

Mind you, there is nothing wrong with marrying a doctor, a professional woman who likes to travel or someone who is well educated, beautiful, successful, handsome or rich. The problem is—as with niceness—these things tell you precious little about who a person really is. And what's even worse, these socially revered trappings of success, career and lifestyle are quite seductive.

Remember, you're not marrying someone's bank account or business card. The chemistry that needs to exist in a relationship must flow from that which makes the person attractive as a person, not that which is alluring about the work they do or how his or her apartment is decorated.

The presence of chemistry is essential to a relationship, and healthy chemistry includes three things:

1. **Love.** You must have strong feelings about this person as a person: his or her inner beauty, virtues and strength of character.
2. **Attraction.** You must feel that this is the type of person you would want to spend time with, grow with and share your life with.
3. **Physical closeness.** You need to feel that you would be comfortable being physically intimate with this person. At the very least this means that he or she can in no way be physically undesirable or a "turnoff." At the same time you don't need to feel wild passion coursing through your veins every moment you are together.

When you've got these three things, you've got chemistry. And chemistry, though not a sufficient basis for marriage, is a necessary ingredient.

Where there is a shared vision of life's goals and genuine love—kindness, loyalty and commitment—then all you need is the slightest pilot light of attraction to know that you have discovered the potential to ignite the flame of marriage—which brings us to our next topic: the role of sex and romance in marriage.

The
Wisdom
of
Sex

− 3 −

The Wisdom of Sex

Love and Sex

*S*himon was invited to present a session at a weekend seminar.

> *George was about twenty-eight and clearly articulated why he had no doubts that love and commitment were not necessary for great sex. A short time later, Arlene, a woman in her mid-fifties, spoke up from the other side of the room.*
>
> *"When I was younger people just didn't talk about things like 'great sex' before they were married; I'm sure none of my girlfriends experienced it." She paused for a moment and looked over in*

George's direction. "However," she continued, "I'm sure there can be great sex without things like love and trust and commitment." And now she looked right at George, "But there is something even greater than great sex—you know what that is?"

"What?" asked George.

"It's great sex accompanied by true love, years of trust and a track record of honesty and commitment." George seemed to blush a bit and was silent.

Postscript: Later in the weekend, Shimon discovered that Arlene was George's mother.

We assume you already know about the birds and the bees, so we won't get into much of that here. Rather, our discussion will focus on what it is that distinguishes what happens in the cozy recesses of the hive from what takes place when a man and a woman embark on the most intimate form of human relationship. In this regard it is important to recognize that all the illustrated manuals, Far Eastern techniques and yoga-esque contortions in the world will never add up to much if you don't have an understanding of what sex is really all about in the first place. Though there is no sex without physical closeness, sex is not physical closeness alone. The heart, the mind and the soul are as essential to physical intimacy as are any other parts of a human being.

Emotions frequently manifest themselves in concrete physical ways. Our bodies undergo observable physiological changes as a result of various emotions we experience internally. What happens to the breathing patterns, the eyes and even the skin of a person who feels afraid or threatened is far different from those of someone who is feeling calm, fulfilled or secure. Similarly, various emotions express themselves in the form of specific actions. A person will have a tendency to act quite differently toward someone whom he or she feels is an adversary than toward someone to whom he or she feels grateful.

Love, the intensely pleasurable emotion experienced by perceiving virtue, goodness and beauty in another human being, seeks to express itself by being close to, or having a relationship with, the one who is beloved. The ways that this closeness is manifested will vary from relationship to relationship.

The Hebrew word for love—*ahavah* —and the Hebrew word for one —*echad* —have the same numerical value. Love seeks to express itself in oneness.

Marriage, as we have discussed, involves a degree of closeness that is different from that of any other love relationship. *"And they shall be as one flesh"* is the description of a type of fusion that is simply unattainable anywhere other than in marriage. The sexual connection between a man and a woman is a vital factor in both achieving and expressing the oneness of marriage.

Sexual relations affect every dimension of the closeness and ultimate union of a man and a woman in their form as one shared being. When the two are inspired by the other's inner beauty and the mutual sense of shared destiny, then the fusion of bodies creates an exalted union whose pleasure is as sensual as it is mystical.

The Definition of Sex

Sex is the physical expression of the bonding of two people who have become one. It is the distinctive language of intimacy and the specialized language of commitment.

The uncommon intimacy and commitment that define a marriage are given dynamic expression in the sexuality of the relationship. Sex means intimacy, commitment and connectedness— always. For sex to engender any other feeling than deep emotional closeness requires a conscious effort to disassociate the physical act from its deep-seated emotional component. As with other experiences, people can, out of choice or necessity, disassociate themselves from the inherent meaning of particular actions. A good salesman, for example, will always try to create a relationship with a prospective customer. As a result, the customer may come to feel that this person genuinely cares about him or his family. Of course in most instances, the salesman has merely gone through the very superficial motions of genuine caring when, in fact, no true relationship or caring was ever intended.

Sex too can be experienced in a way that drains it of authentic emotional content, but this is sex corrupted. The extreme example would be sexual coercion. Here all you have is an empty physical act. What could have been beautiful has become vulgar and disgusting. The same is true when one pays for sex. In this case what you have is a physical act that is just that—an act. In the world of sex for hire, it is precisely the best performers who demand the highest price. This is because they create the illusion that what's taking place is everything that sex is supposed to be and not just a cheap imitation. Even when mature, consenting adults engage in "recreational sex," they too have diminished the sacredness in sex. Recreational sex is all of the motions with none of the emotions. Tennis rackets and skis are recreational items; beautiful body parts are not.

Everyone wants to experience the joy of sex. Paradoxically, when the dominant focus of a sexual relationship becomes sensual arousal and fulfillment, then the ultimate potential for pleasure is immediately compromised. Sex is an intensely intimate form of bonding. To diminish or disregard the element of bonding—of two beings becoming commingled as one—is to deprive sexuality of its very heart and soul. One can surely attempt to deny all this—"To me it's no different from any other physical need," or to ignore it— "Why do you expect him to call just because you made love last night?" But the fact remains: no matter how hard we try to separate the two, sex and profound connectedness go hand in hand. Recognizing this and integrating it into our whole approach to sexuality are the keys to finding our way to the inner garden of one of life's most sublime pleasures.

Sex and Dating

Because sex is the language of intimacy, connectedness and commitment, it can create numerous difficulties when people are dating. Here are four examples of what can happen.

> *"Let's face it," Cathy told Nachum, "we were a storybook couple. Steve was handsome and had an athletic build and a very promising career.There were a lot of women in Los Angeles who would have died for a shot at Steve. And there were a lot of men who would have loved to spend a weekend at my place. I was attractive and intelligent and I knew it . I had also built quite a little business for myself.*
>
> *"Steve and I were convinced that our love was more than just infatuation, and it was. We both felt that there was a deep connection unlike anything either of us had experienced before, and there was.*

Steve was only the second man I allowed to move in with me; the first had been nine years before.

"I remember being at a party once and Steve had a couple of drinks—he wasn't drunk, just looser than usual.

"Something someone said rubbed him the wrong way, and he just lashed into that person. In the middle of a room full of people, Steve just tore this other guy to pieces. There was a vicious look on Steve's face that night. It was a little scary, but I ignored it, excused it.

That was a big mistake. There really is a vicious streak in Steve's personality. Sometimes my life is like a living nightmare."

1. Sexual involvement inhibits critical thinking.

We defined dating as the process by which two people explore the potential for a permanent relationship. And as we saw, nothing is more essential to that process than the ability to perceive and think clearly. When you have sexual relations while dating, it becomes extremely difficult to focus on the primary issues most central to a couple's long-term relationship. For one thing, regular sex is not something that people are anxious to walk away from. The pleasure involved acts as a form of bribery that discourages you from looking too closely at anything that may be an issue serious enough to call the viability of the relationship into question.

Additionally, because sexual involvement brings with it feelings of commitment, there is a part of you that comes to expect permanence in the relationship. When part of you begins to feel like there already is a degree of commitment in the relationship, when the person you're involved with does in fact possess many of the attributes that make him or her a serious candidate for marriage, and when the sex is good, the likelihood of your being up to the challenge of confronting truly difficult questions becomes dramatically diminished. And that's dangerous. A posture of passionate involvement is not the best one from which to evaluate the long-term potential of a relationship.

2. You become more vulnerable.

When you have sex with someone you are dating, you become more vulnerable. Once two people who have been dating for a while have sex, everything changes. The way they look at one another is suddenly colored by the fact that they have experienced an all together different level of intimacy. A shared sexual experience introduces a dynamic that is far different from sharing a dinner, a movie or a walk in the park.

After sex, people want, expect or hope for commitment because that's part of what sex is all about. And though people may try to convince themselves that "the last thing I want now is to make a commitment" or "I just want to have a good time," most people still feel that sex should involve some type of commitment. And when it doesn't materialize, people get hurt. Think about it this way: if the man or woman you have been dating breaks off the relationship shortly after you began having sex, won't you regret the fact that you had sex more than you will regret anything else you did together? And won't the pain of the breakup be more intense now that you have had sex than if it had never happened at all? Sex naturally creates a different degree of connectedness that is all the more traumatic when it is severed.

3. The more people get hurt, the more likely they are to become calloused and cynical.

The more people you date and have sex with, the clearer it becomes that people are quite capable of going through the motions of commitment without being particularly committed at all. It's like when someone you've been dating for a while says, "I love you." The first time you heard those words they stirred a whole set of wonderful feelings, but after years of being disappointed by people who said they loved you, you begin to take those words with a hefty grain of salt. "Okay," you say to yourself, "I've heard that before; now I'll just have to wait and see what's really going on here." The same thing happens with sex. Independent of commitment, sex, though it may be fun, becomes superficial and hollow, and that's exactly how it leaves us feeling.

4. Overuse impairs the language of intimacy.

It is impossible to describe the feelings that parents have at the birth of their first child. But why is that? Why is it that there are no words that can adequately convey what it feels like to hold a moments-old newborn to your breast and nurse for the first time? Why is it that after the birth of a first child so many of us are unable to describe the experience of witnessing the birth? We reach for words like "breathtaking" or "stunning and awesome," but even to our own ears these words sound empty. We have used the word "stunning" so many times to describe things that weren't really so stunning that our words have lost their impact. Language loses its resonance through overuse and misuse. When we most need the words, they are no longer there for us. If everything is awesome, then nothing is awesome.

Sex is the special language of intimacy and commitment. Its unique power and beauty are custom-made gifts that fit perfectly in the context of marriage, the quintessence of loving intimacy and commitment. If you misuse or overuse the language of intimacy, it won't be available when you most want and need to use it. What words will you offer, what tender gesture of closeness will you be able to give to your spouse that you haven't already given to others before? If marriage is a statement that you are entering into a relationship whose bond is different from any other, what part of yourself will you bring to this relationship that hasn't been a part of so many others? What will be the unique expression of commitment, closeness and connectedness that will define this relationship as being unlike any other? This is the role of the language of sex. It communicates a peerless depth of intimacy and commitment precisely when such communication is appropriate, vital and indispensable.

Sex Is Good

Jewish wisdom isn't prudish about sex because the storehouse of Jewish thinking isn't prudish about sex. Throughout the ages Jewish writings have always encouraged couples to find pleasure, harmony and dignity in a sexuality guided by sensitive wisdom. Sex is approached as any other important area of life: with thoughtfulness, frankness and concern for realizing its potential as a vehicle for human fulfillment and ennoblement. Sex is viewed as being holy, pleasurable and beautiful—a wondrous expression of love, depth and commitment. When understood and applied properly, sex becomes a source of vital energy and adds an incomparable, life-enriching dimension to marriage. In short, sex is good.

The Body and Soul of Sex

A hippopotamus is physical, an angel is spiritual and people are somewhere in between. Our experience of existence is that of a blend of disparate elements that seem to have little chance of ever achieving harmony. Yet it is precisely the achievement of symmetry between the physical and the spiritual that remains the challenge of our humanness. Not to glorify the body at the soul's expense, not to elope with the soul and abandon our earthiness, but to achieve a harmonious alliance wherein all parties know when to contribute and when to defer. There is ample room for physicality in the world. There is also space enough for spirituality. For humanness, there is the greatest opportunity of all.

In the Jewish view, life's deepest pleasures are derived from that which expresses the soul and the body in harmony. Unbridled indulgence of the body may feel very good, but it always comes up short in the production of lasting and fulfilling pleasure. Endless titillation of the senses invariably leads to feelings of disgust, not pleasure. And Jewish wisdom sees the purpose of our humanness as being the partaking of the greatest of life's pleasures, not just those that are most easily accessible. It's a gourmet, as opposed to a fast-food, approach to pleasure. This can be said about life just as it can be said about sexuality.

The sexual experience that a married couple shares is meant to expose us to refined layers of pleasure—a pleasure that is rooted both in body and soul. A uniquely human pleasure. Of all the species, only we humans continue to engage in sexual relations after the female has become pregnant. In Jewish life, sexual relations are mandated for a husband and wife regardless of the possibility of procreation. Couples are enjoined to be joined for the sake of pleasures, potentials and meanings that transcend propagation of the species. The experience of shared pleasure is reason enough for a man and a woman to develop a rich sexual life together. In fact, the Talmudic sages, who are legendary for their precise usage of language, use the word *joy* to refer to the act of coitus. This is because sexual relations bring about a feeling of being whole and complete; and wholeness creates joy. Yes, we are capable of mating as any other creature mates. So too we can eat, drink and rear our young as other animals do. Or we can introduce our bodies to our souls and be elevated, dignified and human.

In the area of sexual relations, Jewish wisdom finds little need to regulate the particulars of how or what a husband and wife can or cannot do together. Rather there are two principles that are understood to be the guiding counsels of a couple's sexual expression. The first of these is dignity and the second is privacy.

Dignity and Shame

Beloved is man for he was created in the image of God. This belovedness is especially expressed in man's being made aware that he was created in the image of the Divine.

Chapters of the Sages

A human being who must rummage through someone else's garbage to find his daily sustenance is a tragic figure for a number of reasons. Most tragic of all is his loss of human dignity. Cats and rats and raccoons tear through garbage furiously looking for the leftover scraps of a human meal, and that's okay because they are animals. But when a person has to act like an animal, that's a tragedy.

Human beings are endowed with dignity—not because they walk upright, not because they possess superior intelligence, not because they are capable of composing beautiful music but because they are fashioned in the image of God. Human beings who force other human beings to live and act like animals debase themselves through their attempts to debase another.

Jewish dietary law prohibits the consumption of many types of foods. Nowhere however does it say *"Thou shalt not eat like a pig."* Not that one is allowed to eat like a pig; it's just that it's not included in the dietary laws. Instead, "eating like a pig" is considered a violation of the sanctity and dignity of a human being. When we teach our children to "eat like human beings," we are teaching them far more than socially acceptable table manners. We are teaching them that they are human beings, that there is a special dignity that adheres to their beings and that to compromise that sense of dignity is to tarnish the beloved core of their humanness.

There are unlimited forms of sexual expression. Jewish wisdom finds no shame in the pleasure that one experiences in the marital bed. Far from it. When a man and a woman express their love by tenderly enhancing one another's sexual pleasure, they are engaged in a special means of celebrating their oneness. The shared joy of sexual relations provides a unique voice for their deepest sentiments.

In Jewish life both husband and wife are called upon to learn what brings pleasure to the other and to lovingly care for that pleasure. This is particularly true for husbands. Men, in Jewish marital life, are given a special directive to provide for the pleasure of their wives. This means that a husband needs to resist his inclination for moving too quickly to sexual fulfillment and must be particularly sensitive to his wife's intimate needs, desires and responses. This process of learning how to provide, receive and share sexual pleasures is an important part of married life and serves to draw a couple together in a way that nothing else can. It is in this context that the notion of shame is introduced, and it says; bestow and partake in the sensual pleasures of marriage as you desire—just one thing—don't do anything you would be ashamed of. Anything that is an affront to your dignity or to your spouse's sense of dignity is inappropriate and unacceptable. Just as one should not eat like a pig, one should always be guided by a sense of self-respect—and respect for another—and not act like a pig in bed. Don't allow your passions to drive you to the point where you sacrifice your dignity, and don't ever attempt to push or coerce your spouse to compromise his or hers. It's not right, it's not beautiful and it's not holy. All because it isn't human.

Privacy and Intimacy

A man and a woman can't have an intimate conversation while speaking into a microphone in a room filled with strangers. Even if they were to say the same words and express the same thoughts as they would in private, it could never be the same. What's lost is intimacy, and the reason it's lost is because there is no privacy.

A couple's privacy is a precious commodity that deserves to be carefully tended; and we all recognize this. Imagine that you discovered the presence of someone who was listening in on your most intimate conversations, your most tender moments. Would you not feel deeply violated? But why? Why such horror and outrage? The outrage exists because you have been robbed of a priceless possession—your privacy.

Privacy is a fragile vessel particularly suited to holding an indispensable and irreplaceable dimension of living—that of intimacy.

A couple's privacy is sacred, and its offspring, intimacy, must be inviolable. While shared privacy sets the stage and mood for intimacy, one also needs to be mindful of the need for personal privacy. Whenever a spouse expresses a need for privacy, that need must be respectfully heeded. This type of privacy, as we discussed earlier, implies the creation of boundaries. For the individual, privacy sets limits beyond which you choose not to venture and within which you request that someone else not enter. And so privacy, while it would enable intimacy, would also seem to create distance and separation. But just the opposite is true. The limits of privacy liberate the potential for intimacy. If you have no personal, private, inner core of being, then what of yourself can be shared that isn't already revealed, hasn't already been displayed or hasn't been scandalously pried into? When two people honor one another's privacy, they make possible the shared experience of intimacy.

Sexual Intimacy

The sacredness of privacy is at risk when couples express their passions in the public arena. Jewish wisdom sees the sexual act as being but one point on the continuum of sensual intimacy. Marital relations are like one of those rare and unforgettable conversations that stretch late into the night. In the midst of such a conversation, you reveal parts of yourself and discover parts of another that you never knew before. There is an intense emotional and spiritual crescendo that builds to a glorious and indescribable moment, but this is not a moment that exists in isolation. What preceded that moment—the hours, the words, the gestures—is also a living part of the climactic moment. So too is the gentle descent from that memorable high. And all of it was possible only because the experience was so very, very private.

The same is true for sexual intimacy. Privacy and intensity go hand in hand. The total physical bonding of a husband and wife creates a moment in time when their deepest feelings, their love, joy and ecstacy, are concentrated into a singularly intense experience that transports their relationship to its ultimate plane of existence.

No part of a deeply intimate conversation belongs in the public record, and no part of intimate sexual relations belongs in the public eye. If sexuality is to be an experience of intimacy, then it can't be public. If it is public then it's not intimate, and if it's not intimate, then it is shallow.

The Energy of Exclusivity

Let us now take these notions of privacy and intimacy, together with an understanding that marital relations are meant to be as pleasurable, fulfilling and intimate as possible, and extend our thinking to the area of exclusivity.

Imagine for a moment that you and your husband are the only two members of a space mission that will never return to earth. He is literally the only man in your world. Imagine further that for seven out of every ten days you need to live and conduct your work in separate quarters. And now imagine this. Imagine the intensity of your reunion on the eighth day of each cycle in the mission. Imagine the energy present as the barrier between your quarters begins to open. Imagine that first kiss.

Jewish life strives to make that kiss a reality. And the way to achieve this is by making your spouse the only sensually intimate person that exists in your world.

The art of Jewish sexuality asks you to direct all your sensual energy exclusively to your spouse, the only man or woman in your world. The rewards will be well worth it.

The Power of Separation

Why must a wife separate from her husband for seven days? So that she should always be as precious to him as the day of their marriage.

Babylonian Talmud

One of the most insightful dimensions of Jewish marital life is that of *niddah*. *Niddah* means separation. During a woman's menstrual period, couples enter a time where they pause from physical intimacy. Later, when this time draws to a close, the woman immerses in a specially designed spiritual pool known as a *mikveh*. This is the same pool in which she immersed just prior to her wedding.

The *mikveh* is a source of spiritual rebirth and renewal that has a prominent place in many of Judaism's most significant practices.[8] In the context of marriage, it serves as a portal through which a couple passes on it's way to being reunited. This regular cycle of conscious separation enables a couple to recapture the intensity of their wedding night on a monthly basis.

The cyclical rhythm of separation and renewal created by the *niddah*-separation period works to obviate an inevitable challenge in any marriage—sexual boredom. If sex is the language of intimacy and commitment, then anything that undermines a mutually fulfilling experience will also impair a vital link to a couple's deepest experience of connectedness.

There is a paradox with all physical pleasures. Whatever we enjoy we want more of, yet we know that less is generally better. The finer the restaurant, the smaller the portions. There is only so much pleasure you can draw from a gallon of ice cream or a pound of chips—and once you cross that line, things become nauseating. Gourmands gorge, connoisseurs savor. The same is true in the bed chamber of marriage.

Alongside the inevitable challenge of boredom lies a distinctly American prejudice that often has a corrosive effect on the marital bond. For decades it has been drummed into our heads that *new* is always better. Everything is sold to us because it is "new." An advertisement need not stress what makes a product better because if it's new it *must* be better. And since it is difficult to compartmentalize our attitudes, this association has a tendency to seep into marriage as well. After five, ten or twenty years of marriage, things become all too familiar. It's the same old motions with the same old person. Slowly but steadily the excuses mount for not being able to find special time together. Bit by bit you allow the car you once washed weekly to lose its shine and become rusty. The new models now look so much more attractive and exciting—so much better! So the thought crosses your mind—trade in your spouse for a newer model, or rent one, or borrow someone else's for the weekend.

A regular period of separation provides a mechanism for a husband and wife to rediscover their sexual excitement. Though distant physically, when a man and a woman use this time to express their closeness in other ways, they are constantly reminded how rich and multifaceted their relationship is—or can be. The fact that the relationship continues to grow and mature when sexual intimacy is absent contributes to the feeling that once a month their sexual life is new. Once again feelings of anticipation, excitement and the joy of being husband and wife are injected into their physical bonding. This in turn spills over into other areas of their daily life together— just like it did when they were a young couple.

Another benefit of physical withdrawal is that it enables couples to retain the element of sexual relations as the physical language of intimacy. Often couples can become sexually jaded. After a time only intercourse is still sensual and intimate. Everything else becomes mere camaraderie. A touch no longer communicates anything, a kiss is just another way of shaking hands or waving good-bye. In the Jewish view there is great virtue in maintaining the erotic nature of the whole range of physical contact. A pause in relations not only resensitizes you to the power of relations but also to the whole range of intimate expressions that accompany relations. In the again-exciting atmosphere of renewed intimacy one is reminded of the extraordinary potential of even a touch or a kiss. The experience of reuniting in the most intense way expands the specialized vocabulary of intimacy and closeness available only through the language of arousal, touch and physical bonding.

The Spiritual Bedroom

Wisdom sees no line of demarcation between sexuality and spirituality. A couple's intimacy is as much a part of their spiritual life—their spiritual quest—as is prayer, meditation or an act of human kindness.

There is a quandary present in all endeavors to access spirituality: the apparent existence of a vast gulf separating the finite from the infinite. How can we who are so utterly limited, physical and temporal hope to have any type of contact with a transcendental reality—or "being"—that is boundless, fathomless and wholly independent of time and place?

One of the pathways that seeks to enable us to rise above this barrier involves the cultivation of a sensitized awareness—a keen spiritual eye—that detects in all worldly things a portal to a deeper reality.

> *Nothing exists in the world except the absolute unity which is God. The primary idea of this unity is that, 'the whole earth is filled with His presence.' There is therefore nothing which is devoid of His presence.*

The Baal Shem Tov, first of the Hassidic masters

If one were contemplating a leaf, every line and vein on it take on a major significance. One would see the structure and patterns to which the mind would normally be oblivious. When one uses meditation together with contemplation on a physical object, he can begin to actually see the Divine hidden in the object. The object becomes a channel through which he can experience the Divine.

Aryeh Kaplan [9]

Nothing that exists is unidimensional. God didn't have to create blue skies, tortoises or a moon that reflects but does not shine, but He did. Every element of creation contains a unique lesson, a reflection of the infinite that serves as a passageway to a deeper dimension. Everything that exists—even a leaf—can provide a link to an encounter with God, the source and essence of all things spiritual.

Sexual union is also a channel capable of leading us to an intensely intimate encounter with another human being, as well as with God. The closest Judaism comes to defining God is the statement, *"God is one,"* and when Judaism seeks an image to describe the relationship of a husband and wife it finds itself again at the doorstep of oneness: *"and they shall be as one flesh."* Though we can never fully grasp nor wholly experience the spiritual oneness—the perfect unity of the Creator—there exists a time when we become privy to a glimmer, a taste of this transcendent oneness.

> *A man is required to gladden his wife...to properly prepare her so both should be of one desire and one intent; so that when they join together they will become truly one in body and soul. They become one in soul because they cleave to each other with one will. When they unite in conjugal relations they become one whole unit, one soul, one body—one person. It is precisely then that God rests amongst them in that unified oneness.*

Zohar, Mystical Book of Splendor

This potential for a husband and wife to become bound together, physically and spiritually, creates a unique experience of oneness—of being a single unified essence. Then, together as one, they are capable of sensing the absolute unity present in all things.

Like all forces, sex is a double-edged sword. A knife can be a horrific source of intimidation in the hands of a man threatening your life if you don't hand over your wallet. In the hands of a skilled surgeon, a knife can save your life. Sex is the same way. If misunderstood or abused, it can foster heartbreak and despair, or quite literally, it can be a sublimely creative source of life. Sexual intimacy nourishes love and connectedness and spirituality. And when fully understood, a couple's intimacy can bring them into contact with life's ultimate experience.

The
Wisdom
of
Romance

— 4 —

The Wisdom of Romance

*R*omance is more than confusing; it is doubly confusing. Firstly, many people have a hard time distinguishing between passionate, romantic involvement and love. While romance is an important and powerful dimension of a relationship, it needs to be understood on its own terms and not as a pseudonym for love. Secondly, as we will see, there are two faces to romance: authentic romance and Cupid's romance.

Love and all the romantic images that Cupid's arrow brings to mind are two very different things; in fact, they are not even necessarily related. There can be romance without love, which is usually the case, and there can be love without romance, which is often the case.

Earlier, in "The Wisdom of Dating," we discussed the confounding phenomenon of falling in and out of love. For people who have been actively dating for a number of years, it is quite common to have fallen in love more than once. Similarly, and this is just an extension of what was experienced during singlehood, couples often feel that they have fallen out of love. Worse yet, one or both spouses may find themselves falling in love with someone else.

The source of all the confusion and frustration created by the experience of falling in and out of love lies in a fundamental misunderstanding of what love is, what romance is and what is actually taking place when people fall in and out of love.

Love and Cupid's Idea of Romance

Once again, the definition of love is the pleasurable emotion experienced when one perceives beauty, virtue and strength of character in another human being. For people who are dating and considering potential marriage partners, love is a must. This means that you must derive pleasure and feel a sense of deep admiration for the quality of character that the other person possesses. Love, along with commitment and a shared vision of life's goals, is essential to a meaningful, fulfilling and enduring relationship.

Cupid's romance is something all together different from love. Cupid's romance is the illusion of a meaningful relationship. When two people are romantically involved, their focus is on the more superficial aspects of their relationship. They are concerned more with physical attraction than with inner beauty. Their delight is more in the fleeting experiences of fun, excitement and playfulness than in the mundanity of shared values and goals. Their emotions revel in the ecstasy of the here and now, which demands only the slightest degree of commitment. The seductive illusion of romance is that the passion of the moment can be sustained as the basis for an ongoing relationship. In fact, though their feelings may run as deep as the seas, they are standing on a sandy reef that is just waiting to be washed away.

The Crippling Myth: A Brief History

The whole idea of falling in and out of love is one of the most crippling myths ever embraced by western man. It is based on a misleading conceptual paradigm of love, male-female relationships and marriage, all of which are part of a larger social philosophy known as courtly or romantic love.

The notion of romantic love has its roots in twelfth-century France. Romance began as an elitist form of amusement in the feudal world. It was a kind of social game that was devised by a courtly aristocracy with plenty of leisure time on its hands. Eventually the romantic ideal would go on to capture the imagination of the European masses and shape the way we have related to and pursued love ever since. This new idea of love became *the* idea of love. It was here that love was found to be something that was "blind," a peculiar type of sickness or madness, and was seen as being quite unrelated to marriage. The ideal of "pure love" was recognized not only as being unrelated to marriage but also inherently incompatible with marriage.

We declare and we hold as firmly established that love cannot exert its powers between two married people. For lovers give each other everything freely, under no compulsion of necessity, but married people, on the other hand, have to obey each others wishes out of duty, and can deny nothing of themselves to one another. Therefore, love cannot rightly acknowledge that he has any rights between married people.

Marie, Countess of Champagne
1174

It was at this historical juncture that romantic love became a defining element in western culture. Pure love took on a religious aura that venerated passionate romance and all the attendant feelings of falling in love above all else. Not only was love seen as being incompatible with marriage, but romantic love was also something that was quite acceptable and even laudable in addition to marriage. Marriage, with its merging of assets and the production of children, was a social and economic necessity. "Love," on the other hand, was an intensely celebrated ideal that one longed to experience and around which much of life's aspirations were molded. That a wife might be secretly admired, courted and loved by another man, or that a husband's heart would be hopelessly devoted to another woman, was simply okay. This was not betrayal; this was pursuit of life's loftiest ideal. And this is precisely the point where many of our contemporary problems begin.

If we jump ahead from the medieval origins of courtly love to the present day, we find ourselves struggling to reconcile the irreconcilable. Today extramarital romantic love is not okay. It may be common, but it's not acceptable. Most spouses consider infidelity to be an immoral and unforgivable betrayal. Though we may understand how it can happen and be sympathetic to its causes, we don't, as a society, condone it. We do, however, continue to embrace the idea of romantic love, and that's the killer. Those of us whose idea of love is the romantic idea—and that's virtually all of us—are bent on fitting a perfectly rounded romantic peg in the rather unreceptive square hole of matrimony.

Love is merely a madness, and I tell you, deserves as well a dark house and a whip as madmen do.

Shakespeare, *As You Like It*, 1599

Love is like a fever; it comes and goes without the will having any part in the process...one can only congratulate one's self on the fine qualities of the person one loves as on a lucky chance.

Stendhal, the French novelist, *On Love*, 1830

When you love somebody, you go deaf, dumb and blind.

Robert Redford's assessment of his feelings for Barbara Streisand—*The Way We Were*, 1973

The heart of western man has been conquered by a dreamy notion of love that barely existed before the twelfth century. Granted, the feeling of having someone "madly" in love with you may be quite exhilarating, but do you really want to marry a mad man? And who wouldn't be swept off her feet by someone who confessed to being "lovesick" or "charmed"? But what happens when the "fever" passes? What happens when the charm wears off? Then what?

Falling In and Out of Romance

To the medieval romantic, the instant of falling in love was an epiphany that forever altered the tone and pace of the lovers' every waking moment. At the same time there was an assumption that love generally came with its own form of built-in obsolescence. One of the formal Rules of Love stated that, *"If love lessens, it soon fails and rarely recovers."*[10]

As the modern heirs to the medieval notion of romantic love, we find ourselves wedged into a very tight place. On one hand we are raised with the idea that love has the power to make life worthwhile and that happiness, contentment and love always go hand in hand. And so we dream of finding a perfect love. Yet the romantic warns us: love and marriage are not exactly a perfect fit. What's worse, though your heart may one day find love, you can be assured that it will eventually fade away.

If two people love each other there can be no happy end to it.

Ernest Hemingway—Author and Nobel laureate

If you go away with nothing else from this book, please understand this: people do not fall into love. However, people certainly do fall into the grips of blinding romantic encounters. Because romantic relationships revolve around the superficial and the fleeting—passionate and gripping though they may be—they are inherently doomed to burn themselves out. This is precisely why romantic literature favors tristful tales of a love that is frustrated, unfulfilled or unrealized. It's the Romeo-and-Juliet syndrome—a perfect love, yet a love that is hopelessly unattainable. In Cupid's world it is the very distance, the passionate attempt to turn a doomed rendezvous into a blissful eternity and the intensity of emotion that sanctions no knowledge of anything but the moment that creates the aura and allure of romance. For if the lovers were allowed to have one another forever, then this would surely mean having leftovers for dinner, taking out the garbage and driving the kids to piano lessons, which is hardly romantic. It is, however, what life is all about. It's reality—and romance and reality don't seem to get along.

This is the crux of the problem. When people think they have fallen in love, they haven't. They have fallen into romance. The disastrous mistake is their confusing romance for love. Romance comes and goes—that is its nature. Love is enduring—that is its nature. It is perfectly possible to love someone and feel like killing them at the same time, but you can't be romantic and livid at the same time. The fury kind of puts a damper on things.

When people say they have fallen out of love, as a rule, they haven't. They have fallen out of romance. Again, the confusion of romance for love leads them to conclude that love, one of the cornerstones of a relationship, has vanished. And it hasn't. Only the romantic verve has dissipated, which is okay, because that's what romantic verve does.

People who are capable of distinguishing between love and romance hold the key to keeping both love and true romance alive.

Romance in Marriage

The inescapable need for daily routine has a way of degenerating into a repetitive experience of mundane exercises that squelch our sense of vitality and enthusiasm for life. Consequently we need to be mindful of this tendency and to make an effort to live in a way that we are conscious not only of what we are doing but also of why we are doing it. For this reason Jewish wisdom is full of techniques that strive to capture the extraordinary while it is still clothed in the ordinary.

The marital relationship can easily become caught in the undertow of regularly scheduled events. Here too, that which is beautiful and special becomes dulled by the humdrum cadence of an all too predictable flow of daily routines. This is where the Jewish notion of romance comes in, though it goes by another far less romantic name—honor. Jewish consciousness calls upon a husband and a wife to honor one another like a king and a queen. In other words, we must be aware that there is nothing ordinary about our relationship. If the king or queen were coming to dinner—or even your local mayor for that matter—would you not do things quite differently? Would you not honor the event by adorning it in a manner that reflected the specialness of the occasion?

This is the meaning of authentic romance in marriage. To be romantic is to honor the exalted specialness of the relationship. To honor is to embellish the regular fare of life and transform it into the exceptional. Romantic honor can be almost anything that nurtures feelings of oneness, that highlights the preciousness of the relationship and that reminds a couple how fortunate they are to have one another. The act of honoring the relationship naturally creates a dynamic sense of freshness, excitement and energy.

Authentic romance is a natural expression of—and celebration of—the love and oneness that couples share. Cupid's romance is a counterfeit bill. It's like throwing a party solely for the sake of partying, not to celebrate something important like a graduation, birthday or anniversary. Cupid's romance is in search of oneness. Authentic romance is born of oneness.

The Romantic Getaway

When a man and a woman act to romantically honor their marriage, it's like they are stealing away for a private little vacation. And just like everyone needs to take an occasional vacation, every couple needs to have a romantic component to their marriage. People need to step out of the routine of life. Not because their lives are undesirable or unfulfilling, but simply because a change of pace and scenery is revitalizing. It brings with it the fresh perspective of distance, the soothing balm of leaving the many pressures of life behind and a refueling brought about by enjoying activities that are otherwise locked out of our busy schedules. A good vacation is one that enables you to re-engage life with a refreshed spirit and attitude.

Husbands and wives also need to get away together—if not for a week, then for a night, and if not for a night then for an hour or two. Within a marriage that is built upon a solid foundation of shared values and goals, and deep love and commitment, it is safe to close the door, focus only on the here and now and find delight in a special time stolen away together. It's not only safe, it's wonderful. And contrary to another romantic notion, the less spontaneous it is, the more pleasurable, fulfilling and romantic it will tend to be.

Every couple needs to plan special time together. This time allows them to focus on one another, on the beauty of their relationship and on their oneness. For some this can be a walk in the woods; for others it's a walk around the neighborhood. For some it's a hotel suite; while for others it's sending the kids to grandma's for the weekend and staying at home to do yardwork together.

For some couples a tenderly worded note left in an unexpected place is all it takes to awaken those special feelings. For some it can be watching a video of the first movie they ever saw together; for others, nothing beats flowers.

Regardless of the form—for this will vary from couple to couple—the content of the romantic getaway is one of honor. The practice of creating ways to spend time together is a way of honoring the relationship. Couples who find ways to honor their relationship, and their love, are couples who have discovered a way to nourish a sense of vitality and vibrancy in their life. The romantic getaway says; this relationship deserves reserved special time because it is special. When the king and the queen make dinner reservations, the best table in the house is always reserved for them, whether they request it or not. When a husband and wife reserve a special moment, a special time, place or gesture for one another, then they honor one another as they honor their oneness. And that's romantic.

Down-to-Earth Love

Now that we are able to recognize the difference between love and romance and now that we have an idea of how to create productive romantic intimacy in marriage, let's take one last look at love.

Alas, though our view of love is so "unromantic," it is one that, if accorded its proper due, will spawn a bond of happiness that can last a lifetime. The first step in according love its proper due is to be cognizant of the virtues, beauty and strength of character that your spouse possesses. To begin with, this means taking out a pen and paper and making some lists. (We told you this was unromantic.) Everyone should have some version of the following lists—if not on paper, then at least in your head.

Love List Consciousness

Each of these is a separate list that will contain several items.

List # 1. What do I love about my spouse?

2. What makes her/him special?

3. What is beautiful about him/her?

4. What virtues does he/she possess?

5. What admirable character traits does he/she possess ?

6. What are her/his strengths?

The purpose of these lists is to keep us focused on the things we ought to be focused on. For some reason, people often find it easier to be negative or critical than to be positive and encouraging. This seems to be particularly true with those we are closest with, such as parents, children or spouses. Love-List consciousness helps offset this tendency. This is why it is not only vital to compile our lists but also to review them on a regular basis.

Love-List consciousness does more than just help us overcome our tendency to find faults. It provides a practical technique for confronting the nitty gritty of married life. All marriages experience periods of tension, anger and strife. That's life. The power of Love-List consciousness is that it gives us a secure point of reference that we can always go back to. It's home base, a place from where we can start all over again.

It is also very important (if not downright romantic) to tell your spouse what it is you find in him or her to be so beautiful. Whenever you do this, you send the following message: "I don't take you, or us, for granted. I see, appreciate and deeply admire your inner beauty." The very act of articulation will stir your emotions and arouse your feelings of oneness and love.

Remember, your spouse does possess a great deal of beauty, virtue and outstanding character. And beyond remembering, it is your job to develop a consciousness that identifies your spouse, more than anything else, with the beauty he or she possess.

Shimon often asks people who have siblings the following question: Do you love your brother? The reply is always yes. Then he asks, "Have you ever felt like killing your brother?" Almost always the answer is yes, and from the looks on their faces, some of them really mean it. What we can learn is this: you can feel like killing someone (or throwing something at him, dumping something hot and sticky on his head or calling him all sorts of names) and love him at the same time.

Being conscious of the things you love about your spouse can mean the difference between pulling the trigger or not, even if it's just a water pistol. Love-List consciousness allows you to do more than just cool down; it enables you to regain your equilibrium. It lifts you out of the heat of the moment and puts you back in touch with the bigger picture of your love. It's not a panacea, but such a consciousness will go a long way in restoring peace and harmony when you find yourself falling out of love—OOPS—that's falling out of romance.

Communicating Love with Your Ears

We spoke about every couple's need to romantically honor their relationship by creating specially reserved times to focus on the preciousness of their love and their shared life. One of the most powerful things to do during those times is nothing, other than listen.

Listening is a form of honor. When, instead of talking about yourself, you make an effort to listen to what others have to say about themselves, you send a subtle yet profound signal. When you pay attention and listen to people, you are telling them that they are important, that they matter to you and that you care.

The truth about listening is that it needs to extend beyond just special reserved times. Thoughtful listening needs to be an ongoing part of your daily mode of relating. It needs to be a priority. When you meet at the end of a long day, don't just tell your husband or wife about your frustrations and your ups-and-downs; rather, listen to theirs. Ask him or her, "How was your day?" "Who did you speak to today?" "How are you feeling?" "Did anything unusual or exciting happen today?" Then, just sit back and listen. In marriage, when you listen with your ears, your spouse also hears with his or hers. And what is heard is a voice that says, "I love you."

There also exists another dimension to listening that Jewish wisdom calls *sharing the load*. Sharing the load means to identify with someone else's burdens, to be troubled by his or her troubles. Empathetic listening is a way not only to share a load but also to lighten that load. Often, the best help you can lend someone is to listen. At the same time, sometimes the power of listening just isn't enough to help lighten a heavy load. In that case what you need to do is roll up your sleeves and pitch in. Whenever you take the trouble to help someone with a heavy load, you send a clear message. When that someone is your husband or wife, the message is one of togetherness, concern and love.

Giving, Devotion and Love

The biblical word for love—
ahava—is actually a hybrid formed
from the words *I shall give.*

When the Hebrew word for love, *ahava*, is broken down to its component parts, it is understood to have a dual meaning. Its primary meaning is *I shall give.* The implication here is that giving or being a giving person is somehow intrinsic to what love is all about. The secondary meaning found in the word *ahava* is *I will be given.* The idea here is that love involves a sense of devotedness.

The capacity for giving, for being concerned with and responsive to the needs of others, is arguably the most beautiful of all human traits. It is also one of the most powerful. Recalling that the numerical value of the Hebrew word for "one" (*echad*) and love (*ahava*) is the same, and coupling this with the fact that the word *ahava* also contains within it a call to exercise our capacity to be giving, then what we discover is the following idea. Two people who are committed to being givers possess the basic tools for fostering deep love and a sense of intense oneness.

The dynamics work like this: we live our lives with a sense of possessiveness. There are objects that are ours, time that is ours, property that is ours and thoughts and feelings that are ours. The question is; How do we relate and respond to someone who genuinely needs something that is ours? There exists a reasonable inclination to feel that if I give away that which is mine, then the net result is that I will have less. The truth is, that the gain generally far outweighs the loss. Rather than diminishing what we have, the perspective of devotedness and the act of giving are expansive experiences. When giving is appropriate, then giving of one's self, of one's time, energy or resources, is an act that liberates the possibility for love and connectedness.

In the context of marriage, two people who work to refine their awareness of one another's needs and who make every effort to sensitively respond to those needs are two people who are tilling the rich soil of love. What they soon discover is that rarely does giving result in a loss. Rather, what we are doing when we give of ourselves is planting bits of ourselves in the other. In so doing we become part of one another and are able to more clearly see that our spouse's gain and growth are also our gain and growth. By turning the focus of our hearts toward giving to one another, we actualize our deepest potential as a couple.

In "The Wisdom of Marriage" we said the following: The bond of coupling that marriage creates is one that says "our" needs and "my" needs are interchangeable. Though we are two human beings, there is a dimension of *ourness* that makes us inseparable and indistinguishable. This ourness, this oneness of being, is the key to the most profound and romantic experience of love.

> *Like when one is love sick, and his mind never turns from the love he feels for a woman, and he carries these thoughts with him at all times—when he sits, when he rises, when he eats and when he drinks.*

> Maimonides, 13th century scholar, philosopher, court physician to the Sultan of Egypt, and *hopeless romantic?*

No, Maimonides was not a medieval trouba-
dour singing the ballads of romantic courtly love.
Rather, he was a man who understood the natural
emotions unleashed when two people experience
a merging of essences.

When a husband and wife are devoted to one
another, they are devoted to a larger picture of
who they are as a couple. Jewish wisdom calls
upon every couple to celebrate the passionate
emotional energy created by the fusion of their
beings. How? By being focused on one another,
on their common dreams and on the shared life
they are striving to build. By taking time to notice
and be appreciative of one another's beauty and
by honoring one another with special attention,
affection, words and moments. This cultivating of
their capacity to share, nourish, care about and be
genuinely devoted to one another fills a couple's
identity with a wonderful love and cements it
with sublime oneness. Now how's that for a little
romance?

Cupid, you're fired.

Notes

1) National Center For Health Statistics and The U.S. Census Bureau. Statistics for 1990. Divorce rate of over 50%, 46% of all marriages are a second marriage for at least one of the spouses. Second marriages last an average of two years longer than first marriages. See also: *The Good Divorce*, Dr. Constance Ahrons Ph.D., Harper Collins,1994. *What's Happening to the American Family*, Levitan, Belous and Gallo, Johns Hopkins University Press,1988.

2) *Getting Divorced Without Ruining Your Life*, Sam Margulies Ph.D., Fireside Books,1992.

3) *The Good Marriage*, Judith S. Wallerstein & Sandra Blakeslee, Houghton Mifflin,1995.

4) *If I Knew Then What I Know Now*, Richard Edler, Putnam,1995. (Shimon highly recommends this book)

5) ibid.

6) Genesis 2:24

7) Genesis 2:21, See Commentary of Rashi.

8) *Waters of Eden*, Aryeh Kaplan, NCSY,1982. *Total Immersion*, Rivkah Slonim, Jason Aronson,1995.

9) *Jewish Meditation*, Aryeh Kaplan, Schocken Books, 1985

10) *On the Art of Honorable Loving*, Andreas Capellanus, late twelfth century.

Nachum Braverman
SEMINARS AND LECTURES
(310) 278-8672

"Nachum radiates an enthusiasm to share his knowledge and to promote an introspective thought process. He is truly a brilliant teacher."
Charles E. Hurwitz, Chairman, President & CEO
MAXXAM Inc.

"Nachum takes traditional Jewish wisdom and makes it come alive. I wish his insights and intellectual energy could be packaged and delivered to each and every human being."
J. Morton Davis, Chairman of the Board
D.H. Blair Investment Banking Corp.

"If anyone can teach you how to uncover the meaning you want in life, it's Nachum Braverman. He is not only a wonderful teacher, he genuinely cares about his students."
Cathy Chessler, PR & Marketing Consultant

"Nachum Braverman is one of the most provocative and inspiring teachers in the Jewish world today."
David Wilstein, Past General Chairman, United
Jewish Fund of Los Angeles and President, Realtech
Leasing and Management

"An exceptionally compassionate teacher. He taught my husband and I how to have a productive, meaningful fight."
Susan Weintraub, Homemaker